CW00454809

Lyall Drewett was born in Bristol, England into a devout Christian family. He regularly worshipped at an Evangelical church and in 1958 had the opportunity to study the Scriptures at Emmaus Bible School in America. After two years' study, Lyall returned home and spent several years representing two major companies in the business world. In the 1980s, he became a lay preacher. As a pianist, he made several tapes and discs which were distributed far and wide. Lyall lives in Thornbury, South Gloucestershire and is married to Eleanor with whom he has had three children. Lyall worshipped at Thornbury Baptist Church for almost 27 years and more recently at Old Down Chapel in the village of Old Down, Gloucestershire.

To my dear wife, Eleanor, to whom I am deeply grateful for a lifetime of love and support. I would also like to express my sincere gratitude to Anne and David Ellis for their invaluable help in so many ways in contributing to bringing about the publication of my work. They have devoted so much of their valuable time, giving advice and guidance and at the same time instilling encouragement and confidence which has been so appreciated. I would also like to thank Ian Armour, Eric Pavey and Olwen Wonnacott LRAM for their help in getting the music printed for the hymn I wrote as a prayer for the Holy Spirit's anointing.

Lyall Drewett

THE GIFTS OF THE HOLY SPIRIT

AUSTIN MACAULEY PUBLISHERS™

LONDON • CAMBRIDGE • NEW YORK • SHARJAH

Copyright © Lyall Drewett 2022

The right of Lyall Drewett to be identified as author of this work has been asserted by the author in accordance with section 77 and 78 of the Copyright, Designs and Patents Act 1988.

All rights reserved. No part of this publication may be reproduced, stored in a retrieval system, or transmitted in any form or by any means, electronic, mechanical, photocopying, recording, or otherwise, without the prior permission of the publishers.

Any person who commits any unauthorised act in relation to this publication may be liable to criminal prosecution and civil claims for damages.

The story, experiences, and words are the author's alone.

A CIP catalogue record for this title is available from the British Library.

ISBN 9781398453944 (Paperback)
ISBN 9781398453951 (ePub e-book)

www.austinmacauley.com

First Published 2022
Austin Macauley Publishers Ltd®
1 Canada Square
Canary Wharf
London
E14 5AA

Table of Contents

Background to
the Doctrine

(1 Corinthians Chapters 12,13, and 14.)

Are the gifts of the Holy Spirit for the Church in this dispensation?

I believe that they are and that the Scriptures make it clear that they should be used for the edification of the Body of Christ, which is the Church (1 Corinthians 12:27 – end; Ephesians 4:7–13.) Not only are they for today, but they are also available for all members of the 'Church' endorsing the Biblical teaching of the priesthood of all believers (1 Peter 2:9; Revelation 1:5–6). Having said that they are available for all believers, Scripture makes it clear the Holy Spirit distributes them as he wills and generally speaking, 'different' members of the body of Christ are endowed with 'particular' gifts, but that is never to say that the Lord is unable to give all the gifts to one person should he wish, but of course, that is not how it works out in practice.

There are those who say that the gifts finished at the completion of the Scriptures and base such a theory on 1 Corinthians 13:8 – end, "When perfection comes, the imperfect disappears" (1 Corinthians Ch 13:10).

Some claim that 'perfection' refers to the completed canon of Scripture, but it is abundantly clear from the context that no such meaning is intended, and furthermore, Paul goes to great lengths to give instructions on the use of the gifts and their benefits to the Church particularly in 1 Corinthians Chapters 12 and 14. It is patently obvious that the 'Church' is still in existence, and the gifts of the Holy Spirit have been appointed by God "in the Church" (1 Corinthians 12:28).

The Church didn't stop existing when the apostles died, praise the Lord, and neither did the gifts. It is significant too that the Prophet Joel speaks of the outpouring of the Holy Spirit in a manifestation of the gifts such as prophecy, visions and dreams in the last days before the coming of Christ, and these signs are obviously after the completion of the canon of scripture (Joel 2:28; Acts 2:14 etc.). It is not without significance too that the fastest growing 'denomination' in the Christian Church is the Pentecostal 'wing' and those churches who seek to use the Gifts of the Spirit and believe in the baptism of the Holy Spirit.

The fact that the Apostle Paul devotes so much time and uses so many Scriptures clarifying the correct use and employment of the gifts in 1 Corinthians, Chapters 12 and 14 and encourages his readers to "earnestly covet the best gifts" (12:31) and "eagerly desire spiritual gifts especially the gift of prophecy" (14:1) is not without significance and importance.

The gifts of the Holy Spirit existed before the day of Pentecost when individuals and groups of God's people were empowered by the Holy Spirit i.e., The Spirit fell on Gideon (Judges 6:34), Samson experienced the power of the Spirit when he tore a lion apart with his bare hands (Judges 14:6), and the 70 Elders in the wilderness prophesied when the Spirit came upon them (Numbers 11:24–25 etc.). However, the presence of the Spirit as a permanent possession of the believer did not take place until Pentecost. Christ himself exercised the gifts, and his prophetic ministry is seen in such passages as John 4:18–19. As we are well aware, Christ was a miracle worker, and his healing ministry knew no bounds. He gave his disciples power to heal and cast out demons and even to raise the dead (Matthew 10:8) before Pentecost, but they were to be empowered with 'power' from on high to enable them to witness more effectively and accomplish even greater things after Christ's return to the Father (John 14:12; Acts 1:8).

How do we receive the Gifts of the Spirit?

As we have seen above, we should, as believers, have a thirst for spiritual gifts because we constitute the body of Christ, and our individual gift, whatever it may be, is to be used for the 'common good' of God's people. We should, therefore, ask the Lord firstly to baptise and fill us with His Holy Spirit to equip us for service amongst his people and in the world. It is only as we are filled with his Spirit that we are truly able to acknowledge his Lordship over our lives and allow his Spirit to flow through us in blessing to our brothers and sisters in Christ (1 Corinthians 12:1–7,13; John 7:37–39).

As the Holy Spirit fills us, He will give us, as He determines, the right gift for us individually (1 Corinthians 12:8–11). It does not mean that the gift we receive will necessarily 'suit' our particular personality because God is sovereign and is able to do "abundantly above all that we ask or think according to the power that works within us" (Ephesians 3:20). What we may think is our 'natural' gift is not necessarily what our 'spiritual' gift may be.

All the gifts of the Spirit are important, but the Apostle Paul does put emphasis on the gift of prophecy. This may well be because it is seen as "God speaking to his people for their strengthening, encouragement and comfort" (1 Corinthians 14:1–3) and causing those who hear to know that the Lord is speaking to them personally (1 Corinthians 14:24–25). However, not every believer is a prophet, although 'potentially' God is able to give any of the gifts to any person should he wish to do so at any time.

Having said that, generally speaking, God gives different gifts to different people because he does things in an orderly manner (1 Corinthians 12:27 – end), and each 'member' of the Body is a vital constituent (1 Corinthians 14:40).

The gifts are a vital part of our private and corporate lives as Christians inasmuch that their purpose is for the edification of ourselves and the whole of the body of Christ.

Let us seek the Lord earnestly that, by his grace, he will impart his gifts to us. When the Holy Spirit first came on the disciples at Pentecost, "they began to speak in other tongues as the Spirit enabled them" (Acts 2:4). "Be filled with the Spirit" (Ephesians 5:18; John 7:37–39).

Do not be afraid to exercise your gift but reach out in faith in the power of the Spirit, and he will use you mightily. We are told that Christ gives gifts to men (Eph 4:8), and whilst we may ask for a particular gift and are encouraged to do so, it is 'through the Spirit' that the gifts are given, and he distributes them "severally as he wills" (1 Corinthians 12:11).

The 'gifts' (Greek word charisma) are an expression of God's grace, favour and kindness. Do not spurn what God has freely made available to us, but through prayer and earnest supplication may we apprehend, in faith, what the Lord wants to give all of us and may the glory go to Him alone.

Apostles

(1 Corinthians Ch 12 Vs 27 – end)

'Apostles' are included in the list of the gifts of the Holy Spirit mentioned in Ephesians 4:7–13, as well as the verses listed above. The gift of 'apostleship' is linked to the gift of 'prophecy' as being 'foundational' gifts in the Church (Ephesians 2:20). The Greek word for apostle means 'One sent forth'. Generally speaking, when we speak of apostles, we think of the original 12 with whom Christ chose to work and whom he trained to help him in his ministry of breaking new ground in preaching the Gospel of the Kingdom and healing the sick etc. I was always led to believe that the main qualification of being an apostle was to have been with Christ from the time of John's baptism up to the ascension and to have been a witness with the other apostles of the resurrection (Acts 1:21–22).

Certainly, these verses support such teaching, but a deeper study of the scriptures and an understanding of the reference to 'apostles' in the list of those who constitute the members of the 'Church' in 1 Corinthians 12:28 puts a different perspective on the subject and other references to apostles who are clearly not "one of the 12", shows that a broader understanding of the title and ministry of an apostle is imperative.

The gift of 'apostleship' is very different from all the other listed gifts of the Spirit inasmuch as it is a gift which is conferred on a person by God and not so much a gift which can be sought or desired. It is the commissioning of God on a person and a calling to a specific work or ministry for Him. Thus, the Apostle Paul, in his salutations to the various churches, to which he wrote mentions his calling to be an apostle and even clarifies his position by stating that he had been sent not from men, nor by man but by Jesus Christ and God the Father (Galatians 1:1).

Clearly, Paul in his epistles frequently refers to himself as an apostle and uses the expression in the following salutation to the Church at Corinth. "Called to be an Apostle of Christ Jesus, by the will of God." (1 Corinthians 1:1). His calling was specifically to reach the '"Gentiles" with the Gospel, and he planted several Churches in Asia Minor and Europe, whilst Peter's calling was to reach the Jews primarily; both were called and 'sent forth' as apostles of Christ for these ministries. When writing to the Thessalonians in his first letter 2:6 and 1:1, Paul refers to himself, Silas and Timothy as apostles of Christ.

Also, in Philippians 2:25, Paul refers to Epaphroditus as 'your messenger' and the Greek word used here is translated in other passages as 'apostle'. However, we know that none of these was one of the original 12, and neither were some of Paul's relatives who are also designated 'apostles' in Romans 16:7.

As the apostles laid the foundation of the early Church so, in these days of apostasy, we need apostles who are called of

God to help repair the crumbling foundations of the Church, which has come under so much attack from the enemy, particularly in the past 100 years. False biblical teaching, which does not conform to the apostles' doctrine, has infiltrated the Church, and the foundations need rebuilding and strengthening. There is a need for apostolic input in the form of sound teaching by Spirit-filled men who have been called of God to fulfil such a ministry.

Down through the ages, God has had his apostles, and in our own day, we need people like Hudson Taylor, who was sent by God as a missionary to China and founded the China Inland Mission 1866. This mission was responsible for bringing 800 missionaries to the country and directly resulted in 18000 conversions! One could mention many more who were sent by God to accomplish great things for his Kingdom and eternal glory.

It is very important to recognise that the Lord Jesus Himself is called The Apostle and High Priest whom we confess (Hebrews 3:1)

Time and time again, Jesus reminds His hearers of His commission by His Father, having been 'sent' to the lost sheep of Israel (Matt 10:40,15:24; Mk 9:37; Luke 9:48; Jn 4:34, 5:24,30,36–38, 6:38).

It is important to understand that in spite of what has been mentioned so far, the 12 original Apostles were 'special' in the sense that Christ personally called them whilst on earth, and they were privileged to have learnt the scriptures and issues of the kingdom first hand from their blessed Master and to have beheld His glory, the glory as of the only begotten of the Father full of grace and truth (2 Peter 1:17–18)

The use of the definite article when speaking of the 12 indicates their special position as apostles, and a reference to them in the book of Revelation 21:13–14 also gives them particular recognition.

In Ephesians 2:20, Paul explains that the Church, of which all members are a part, is built on the foundation of the apostles and prophets. This refers to the founding work of the apostles and prophets as they preached and taught God's word (1 Corinthians 3:10–11). It should be clearly understood that the apostles and prophets laid the foundation, but Christ is the 'chief cornerstone'.

When Peter made his confession at Caesarea Philippi that Jesus is the Christ, the Son of the living God, (Matthew 16:18), Jesus replied, "Thou art Peter (*Petros* from the Greek meaning stone), and on this Rock, (*Petra* from the Greek meaning rock) I will build my church and the gates of hell will not prevail against it." The true foundation of the church is Christ, the rock, not Peter, the stone. Peter himself, in his first epistle, calls the church a 'spiritual house' and each believer is called a 'living stone' and is being built into this spiritual house.

There is a need, especially in these days, to recognise that there will be an infiltration of "false Apostles" in the church. The Apostle Paul warned sarcastically about them in 2 Corinthians 11, where he refers to them as "Super-Apostles." In verse 13, they are described as deceitful workmen, masquerading as apostles of Christ. Their end will be what their actions deserve.

Apostleship is a 'spiritual' calling of the Lord, and those called to such service will know that they have been appointed by the will of God (1 Corinthians 1:1; Acts 9:15). God sent

Ananias to Paul after his conversion to tell him he had been called to be sent forth as his chosen instrument to carry his name before the Gentiles and their kings and before the people of Israel. This prophecy was totally fulfilled in Paul's life and specifically his defence before King Agrippa. Peter was sent by God to be an apostle primarily to the Jews. It is a fact, of course, that all Christians have been 'called' and 'chosen' by God to become part of His body, the Church, and to play their part in it through the exercising of the gifts of the Spirit (Jude 1:1; 1 Corinthians 12:7; 1 Peter 2:9). However, 'apostleship' is a specific calling to a particular ministry in the Church, often involving the breaking of new ground in preaching the Gospel, Church planting and teaching.

The 12 Apostles received 'specific instructions' from Christ through the Holy Spirit, after his resurrection and before his ascension, indicating the importance of their status in the 'forthcoming' Church which was about to be inaugurated (Acts 1:2).

What are some of the things that characterise an Apostle?

They possessed amazing 'prophetic revelation', and Peter exercised this gift when the Holy Spirit revealed to him the fact that Ananias and Sapphira had kept back some of their money from the sale of a property for themselves instead of giving it to the apostles as the other believers had done. Acts 5:1–11 their deaths followed because they had lied to the Holy Spirit.

2 Corinthians 12:12 speaks of those things which have the mark of an apostle i.e., signs, wonders and miracles.

Acts 5:12–16 The apostles performed many miraculous signs and wonders among the people. All who came to them were healed.

Peter, in his sermon on the day of Pentecost, speaking of Jesus, says, "Jesus of Nazareth was a man accredited by God to you by miracles, wonders and signs."

Outward evidence of God's commissioning of the apostles manifested itself in an authority seen in the power of the Holy Spirit being imparted for various ministries within the Church, such as Church government, teaching, the laying on of hands for the baptism in the Holy Spirit, the receiving of spiritual gifts and a calling to specific ministry (Acts 8:14–17; 2 Tim 1:6).

At the council at Jerusalem in Acts Chapter 15, Paul and Barnabas were appointed along with some other believers to go to Jerusalem to settle a dispute over false teaching from some men who were converted Pharisees and had insisted on Gentile believers being circumcised before they could become true Christians.

Apostles worked alongside the Elders in the Churches and their authority was put on the same level as the Old Testament Prophets by Peter in 2 Peter 3:2.

As with many of the gifts of the Spirit, the gift of Apostleship can overlap, and other gifts can flow from it. Paul reminds Timothy of his gift of 'preaching' in his first letter 2:7, where the word preacher is rendered herald in the authorised translation. As with many gifts of the Spirit, an apostle will often have several 'giftings', and Paul speaks of himself as an "Apostle, Preacher and Teacher of the true faith" (1 Tim 2:7).

Let us pray that God will raise up in our day apostles who will bring restoration to the wounded Church and honour to the name of Jesus.

Discernment

(1 Cor Ch 12 V 10) (1Cor Ch 14 v 29)

There are four Greek words which are translated discern, discerner and discernment in the New Testament. The first is '*anakrino*'. This same word is also translated judge and examined in several verses, many of which are referred to in the following notes. It also means to distinguish or separate out so as to investigate (*krino*) by looking throughout objects or particulars, hence signifies to examine, scrutinise, question, to hold a preliminary judicial examination preceding the trial proper. This first examination implying more to follow, is often present in the non-legal uses of the word, e.g., Luke 23:14 here the word is used regarding Pilate's examination of Jesus and his conclusion that he had no basis to bring a charge against him. Also, figuratively 1 Cor 4:1–3.

In Acts 17:11, when Paul and Silas were in Berea and preached the word, the Bereans received the message with great eagerness and examined the Scripture, exercised spiritual discernment to see if what Paul said was true. How important this is today when there is an increasing infiltration of false teaching and 'heresy' coming into the Church that we test the validity and source of the things we are being taught. Determining the excellence or defects of a person or thing also requires discernment, and Paul stresses this fact when he speaks about the 'natural' man without the Spirit who is unable to discern that which is of the Spirit in 1 Cor 2:14.

The second word is '*diakrino*', which means to separate, discriminate, to determine, to decide. In Mathew 16:3 and Luke 12:56, this word is used when Jesus challenged the Pharisees because they thought they were able to discriminate between the varying conditions of the sky, but they lacked the discernment to recognise the signs of spiritual crisis, the coming of the Messiah, the threat of his death, the coming confrontation with Rome and the eternal consequences these events would have for their own lives. 1 Cor 11:29 in the context of the Lord's supper by not discerning or discriminating as to what the 'elements' represent and their Holy Significance. In 1 Corinthians 14:29, the same word is used of 'weighing' (the word 'judge' is used in the AV) what is said in prophecy so that its content may be tested as being of the Holy Spirit.

Another word is '*diakrisis*'. It means a distinguishing, a clear discrimination, discerning, judging, and is translated discerning in 1 Cor 12:10, of discerning or distinguishing of spirits, judging whether they are evil or of God. In Hebrews 5:14, a phrase is used which is concerned with having the ability of discriminating between good and evil through sound and 'mature' Bible teaching; what the writer of Hebrews calls solid food, as opposed to the milk of the word. In Romans 14:1, the same word is used in the sense of exercising discernment in our 'judgement' of a weaker brother or sister's scruples.

Kritikos is an adjective and only found once in the New Testament. It signifies that which relates to judging, fit for, or skilled in judging, and it is found in Hebrews 4:12 where it is speaking about the 'Word of God' (the Scriptures). "For the Word of God is living and active; sharper than any double-edged sword, it penetrates even to the dividing of soul and spirit, joints and marrow, it judges the thoughts and attitudes of the heart." As the word is preached, its discerning influence through the work of the Holy Spirit can accomplish mighty things in our lives and all those who come under its authority.

Summary

Discernment is a very important gift of the Holy Spirit and is equally as relevant and needful in the church today as it was in the days of the early church, if not more so! There has probably been a greater increase in the number of false 'sects' infiltrating the church in the past 100 years than at any time since the day of Pentecost. The gift of discernment is a vital means in being able, through the power of the Holy Spirit, to distinguish between what is of God, in terms of teaching, prophecy, the spirits, and 'people' who may be bringing false teaching into the church. There is a sense in which all Christians have the gift of discernment, and it is through the presence of the Holy Spirit in the life of the believer that he or she is able to 'spiritually discern' what God has given them (1 Cor 2:8 – end).

Sometimes discernment may manifest itself through the ministry of the Holy Spirit giving a clear 'revelation' through a vision, a dream or other means, to expose the presence of a person who may be, for example, involved in the occult and is bringing seriously false and heretical teaching into the Church. It might be thought that such false and demonic teaching should be easily recognised by 'discerning' Christians, but we must not forget that even Satan himself can be transformed into an angel of light and even the very elect of God can be deceived, as will be the case during the tribulation (2 Cor 11:14; Matthew 24:23–25).

Hereunder are some passages of Scripture which warn about false teaching entering the Church, and such verses make us realise the importance of the gift of discernment in enabling us to establish that what is being taught is biblically sound.

(Acts 20:28–31; Col 2:4–8, 18; 2 Peter 2:1–3; 1 Tim 4:1–11; Hebrews 5:12 – end; 1 John 4:1–6).

Healing

Matthew Ch 10 verses 1–8

1 Corinthians Ch 12 verses 27–31

The 'gifts' of healing are mentioned in 1 Corinthians 12:9, 28 but not in the list in Ephesians 4:11.

Let us state at the outset that "Our God is a healing God."

I'm sure that all of us can testify to the Lord's healing power over the years in our own lives and those of other believers. God's name in Exodus 15:26 (Jehovah-Rophi) is an early reminder in Scripture that our God is a mighty healer. In this context in the Old Testament, God's people were rewarded for seeking to listen to his voice, doing what was right in his eyes and paying attention to his commands and keeping his decrees.

Interesting that the gift in the New Testament is in the plural and so could imply healing of diverse illnesses or the possession of the gift by more than one person in the fellowship. The gifts of healing are mentioned in the list of the other gifts of the Holy Spirit, and their operation should take place as the Spirit leads. When the church meets together, it could be that a prophetic revelation enlightens a healer's awareness to a particular need for healing, or a person requiring healing may feel that the Spirit is leading them to request prayer for a particular illness. I don't believe that 'healing meetings' should be the order of the day, generally speaking. There is no such illustration from scripture of such 'meetings' taking place, and when they do, in this day and age, they sometimes draw more attention to the healer than the healing itself, and there is the danger of 'exhibitionism' and self 'exultation'. However, I believe there are situations in the course of everyday life where the gifts of the Spirit will be manifested and are readily available to meet any particular need as it arises. This was unquestionably the case in our Lord's life and ministry.

A biblical procedure to be followed is outlined in James 5:13–16, where the invitation is given by James for the person who is 'sick' (Greek word meaning infirm, or without strength) to call for the elders of the church that they may anoint the sick with oil and pray for healing in the name of the Lord. Anointing with oil for healing is also mentioned in Mark 6:13. In ancient times olive oil was used to soothe and bring healing to wounds, such as in the case of the good Samaritan who 'poured on oil and wine' on the wounds of the man who had been attacked on the road from Jerusalem to Jericho.

Luke 10:34; Isaiah 1:6 also refers to the healing properties of oil. Reference to these incidents is in no way to detract from the undoubted healing power of our omnipotent God. It is stated that the "prayer offered in faith will make the sick person well; the Lord will raise him up." This is clearly not what always happens and, so one needs to analyse the content of these verses in the light of scripture as a whole. We must recognise the principle that no biblical teaching or doctrine should be based on a single verse of Scripture. We must also recognise the sovereignty of God in all prayer.

We are familiar with the prayer of Christ himself in the garden of Gethsemane when he asked his Father, "If it is possible, take this cup from me nevertheless, not my will but Thine be done." God's will is at the very heart of the Lord's prayer, and it is only as we pray 'according to his will' that he hears us and, in doing so, we know that he hears us and we know that he will grant us what we have asked of him (1 John 5:14–15). It is important to recognise that the holiness of life, including obedience and seeking to please the Lord, are prerequisites to answered prayer (1 John 3:21–22). Our faith is also a vital part of the prayer being made on behalf of the sick person.

Peter, in his first epistle, makes it very clear that part of our Spiritual maturity is the 'testing' of our faith in all kinds of trials so that it may be proved to be genuine and ultimately result in praise, glory, and honour when Jesus Christ is revealed. If our faith is to be tested, it has to go through the fire as gold in its refining process, and this can mean varying kinds of trials such as a particular prayer not being answered in the way we expected it, or experiences of life such as bereavement or tragedy of some kind. The 'goal' of our faith is the salvation of our souls, and it should be this prospect that causes us to greatly rejoice in whatever trials we are called to go through (1 Peter 1:6–9).

It is also very important too, to realise that God's chastening in our lives is part of his 'agenda' of corrective and instructive training for our development as his children. Far from being a reason for despair, discipline is a basis for encouragement and perseverance (Hebrews 12:7–12).

The Apostle Paul prayed three times that "his thorn in the flesh" would be healed, but his request was not granted; however, he was given the assurance from the Lord that "His Grace is sufficient for His Strength is made perfect in weakness" (2 Cor 12:7–10). It seems likely that the apostle is talking about a 'physical' illness in view of his reference to "weakness" and the fact that he refers to having to write in 'large' letters and mentions an 'illness' in his epistle to the Galatians 4:13 and 6:11.

It is 'noteworthy' to read in Mark 6:5 that Jesus was unable to work any 'miracles' because of the people's lack of faith and was only able to heal a few folk! There are many incidents throughout the New Testament where, in connection with healing, faith is mentioned as being a necessary 'component' of the healing process, not only on the part of the healer but also on the part of the one being healed. However, it is imperative to stress that at the end of the day, there have been many devoted and 'faith-full' believers who have sought the Lord for healing which has not been forthcoming, and we need to recognise God's sovereign will in all our requests and have the spiritual insight and maturity to be able to discern the will of God and accept it without question.

I know it has been said many times before, but it is relevant and bears repeating to say that "if everybody who is sick and is prayed for is always healed, then we would never die", nor would we know possibly what the testing of our faith really means. We must also remember that God is not in the habit of reversing the ageing process (Psalm 90). The Scriptures make it plain that the outward man is perishing, but inwardly we are being renewed day by day (2 Cor 4:16).

It's also worth noting that the Apostle Paul then goes on to say, "For our light and momentary troubles are achieving for us an eternal glory that far outweighs them all." So, we fix our eyes not on what is seen but on what is unseen. For what is seen is temporal, but what is unseen is eternal. It reminds us of those wonderful words of Paul in Romans 8:18 "I consider that our present sufferings are not worth comparing with the glory that will be revealed in us."

It's also worth remembering that Revelation speaks about Heaven and reminds us that "there will be no more pain, tears or death for the former things have passed away" (Revelation Ch 21). Most of us, when we are called to glory, will inevitably take some of our earthly ailments with us, but the Scriptures assure us that the former things will have passed away. Total healing due to being clothed with our 'Heavenly dwelling' will ensure our 'total' healing one glorious day (2 Cor 5:2).

And we will be with Christ forever... Oh, how wonderful; Oh, how marvellous! And my song shall ever be, Oh, how wonderful, Oh how marvellous, is my saviour's love to me! Even so, come Lord Jesus.

Miracles

1 Cor Ch 12 Whole Chapter

Miracles, as with the other gifts of the Holy Spirit, are mentioned in 1 Cor 12:10, 28–29. However, they are not on the list in Ephesians Ch 4. The gift is called "miraculous powers" and "workers of miracles". Miracles are listed separately from "gifts of healing" in 1 Corinthians 12:9 because they are a totally different gift and are often not about 'healing' at all but are miraculous demonstrations of God's supernatural power which may be manifested in varying miraculous occurrences, for example, the deliverance of Paul and Silas and subsequent deliverance of Peter from prison, (Acts 12, 16 – end) were both miracles of divine intervention, and there are countless occasions in Scripture when God intervened in the lives of his people and their enemies, in miraculous power, deliverance and sometimes judgement. Some are referred to later in these notes. Another significant distinction between miracles and the other gifts is that they take place sometimes independently of any involvement of a member of the body of Christ, such as in the case of the prophecy of Joel in 2:30–31 referred to below and many others.

There are two main words used in Greek which are translated miracles, one meaning 'power' (*Dunamis*) and the other 'signs' (*semeion*). In the Revised Version (the revised, mid-nineteenth-century English translation of the King James version of 1611), the word 'Miracle' in the synoptic Gospels, in every occurrence, with the exception of Luke 23:8, is substituted by the word 'Signs'. Thus, the predominant word for miracles is 'signs'. Even the word 'wonder' in the book of Revelation (Rev 12:1–3, 13:13) is the same Greek word '*semeion*' (above; signs) although the main word used for a wonder is '*teras*' which means something strange, causing the beholder to marvel and it is always used in the plural.

Miracles, wonders, and signs are often grouped together to describe a manifestation or display of the supernatural power of God performed by Christ and his apostles, and they are still potentially available for the church today. However, in Acts 2:19, the word 'wonders' occurs alone where Peter is quoting from Joel's prophecy concerning the outpouring of the Holy Spirit in the "last days" prior to the second coming of our Lord Jesus. Joel speaks of wonders in Heaven above and signs on the earth, astronomical happenings in the heavens and wonders on the earth.

It may be helpful to recognise that a 'sign' is intended to appeal to the understanding, a 'wonder' appeals to the imagination, and a 'miracle' (*Dunamis*-power) indicates its source as supernatural.

In the Old and New Testaments, God used miracles as a sign of his presence with his people and his divine authority; they were also a confirmation of his love and faithfulness to them and an assurance of his power with them against their enemies. The words used in the Old Testament for miracles are 'signs' and 'wonders'. In Isaiah 35:5 – end, the prophet speaks of the miracles (signs) which would accompany the coming of the promised Jewish Messiah. The Apostle Peter reminds his hearers on the day of Pentecost of Christ's fulfilment of Messianic Prophecy through the working of miracles, wonders, and signs (Acts 2:22).

Jesus rebuked the Pharisees and the teachers of the law because of their insistence on seeing a miraculous 'sign' and called them "a wicked and adulterous generation" for making such a request. He called them "adulterous", not meaning physical adultery but spiritual, as they had become unfaithful to their spiritual husband, namely God (Matthew 12:38–40). In spite of their knowledge as teachers of the law, they didn't have the discernment to recognise the significance of the 'miracle' of Jonah and the huge fish as a type of Christ and its prophetical yet future fulfilment in the death and resurrection of Jesus.

Many of the miracles which Christ performed took place to demonstrate various aspects of his Deity, and, as such, they testified to the fact that he was truly the Messiah.

Christ's miraculous healing of the lame man lowered through the roof of a house was a 'sign' of his divinity to prove that he had the authority and power to forgive sin, and only God can do that! (Luke 5:17–39).

Christ's feeding of the 5000 was a 'sign' of his true nature as the spiritual 'bread' of life, made clear in his discourse on the subject following the miracle in John Ch 6.

The raising of Lazarus from the grave was a 'sign' of the Deity of Jesus as the author and sustainer of life and Victor over death and the grave (John 11).

In Mark 6:5–6, we read that Jesus was unable to perform any miracles in Nazareth because of the people's lack of faith. We must be careful if involved in healing ministry about questioning people's faith or lack of it. Let us not forget that Jesus knew in his omniscience that the people lacked faith in this particular instance; even so, he was able to heal a few folk, so they don't appear to have been faithless!

I believe that we may be misguided in our understanding for the 'reason' or 'purpose' of a miracle, inasmuch that such an event is not intended to be seen as a 'conjuring' trick for the enjoyment of all observers but rather a manifestation of the power, presence, and sovereignty of God, and a sign for His glory alone.

Miracles often take place as a 'sign' or 'confirmation' of God's approval at a given time in our work and ministry for him (Mark 16:19–20). After Christ's ascension, the disciples preached everywhere, and the Lord worked with them and proved that their preaching was true by the miracles that were performed.

Immediately after Pentecost, the Lord confirmed the promise of his power and presence in the many wonders and miraculous signs which were done by the apostles (Acts 2:43). The healing of the lame man outside the temple was a case in point (Acts Ch 3). The people came running to the temple to hear Peter as he preached of Christ the Messiah and the power of His name. Throughout the book of Acts, God was constantly manifesting the endorsement of His 'blessing' on the apostles' ministry by continuing to perform miracles, signs, and wonders (Acts 5:12, 6:8). In Acts 14:3, when Paul and Barnabas were in Iconium in the Jewish synagogue, many Jews and Gentiles came to believe in Christ, but there was

33

considerable opposition from Jews who would not believe the message. However, Paul and Barnabas spent considerable time speaking boldly for the Lord, who confirmed the message of His grace by enabling them to do miraculous signs and wonders.

The two words used in the New Testament are 'signs' and 'power'; the second word being the identical word used by Christ when speaking of the day of Pentecost and the power the disciples would receive when the Holy Spirit was poured out on them (Acts 1:8)., (the Greek word being *dunamis*). Predominately miracles were performed as 'signs' to draw attention to the omnipotence of God and thus cause the enemies of the Lord and his people to recognise his sovereignty and the nature of his character and person. Many miracles were a demonstration of God's judgement on individuals and nations.

In Acts Ch 5, we read of the death of Ananias and Sapphira, who were 'miraculously' struck dead because of their deceit in holding back profit from the sale of a property which should have been brought to the apostles. In Exodus 7:8–13, we read of the miracle of Moses' staff becoming a snake and swallowing up the counterfeit snakes of the Egyptian magicians before Pharaoh, a sign of God's power and presence with his servants. Numbers Ch 16, the destruction of Korah, Dathan and Abiram, who rose up against Moses. God's judgement was also manifested by the miracles he used against Pharaoh when he killed all the firstborn Egyptian sons and ultimately parted the waters of the Red Sea to bring about the deliverance of his people Israel.

It's important to recognise too that the evidence of miracles is not necessarily proof that they have originated from the Holy Spirit, and we need to remember that even Satan can be transformed into an angel of light and Christ warned that in the last days, even the 'elect' of God will be deceived by miracles which will take place performed by false Christs and prophets (Matthew 24:24).

Jesus warned his disciples that "not everyone who calls me Lord will enter the kingdom of Heaven but only those who do the will of my Father." He then goes on to say, "many will say to me, Lord, Lord! In your name, we spoke God's message, by your name; we drove out many demons and performed many miracles!" Then I will say to them, "I never knew you depart from me, you wicked people" (Matthew 7:21–23).

Let us be a people who recognise and acknowledge that our God is a miracle-working God and nothing is too hard for him. At the same time, let us not forget that he is sovereign, and his will must be the ultimate objective in every aspect of our service for him. To this end, may we remain faithful, diligent, vigilant and expectant, looking for the 'signs' following our ministry for the Lord and to him alone may all the glory be given.

Pastors

The word pastor occurs eight times in the Old Testament, and every reference is in the book of Jeremiah where the meaning is 'to feed'.

Whilst the Hebrew word *partic* is translated as pastors, all modern translations of the Bible, including the N.I.V, render the word shepherd with one exception viz; Jeremiah 2:8 where it is translated as leaders. However, even the word leaders is more accurately Shepherds according to concordances and the N, I.V. Study Bible notes. References in Jeremiah where the Hebrew word *partic* is translated as shepherds in the modern translations, as opposed to pastors, in the authorised Bible, are as follows; Ch 3:15, 10:21, 12:10, 17:16, 22:22, 23:1, 23:2.

In the New Testament, the word is only found once, and its meaning is shepherd or feeder, from the Greek word '*poimen*'. The word for Shepherd is one who tends herds or flocks (not merely one who feeds them), and it is used metaphorically of 'Christian' pastors in Ephesians 4:11.

In this passage, Paul lists the five gifts Christ gave to equip and edify his Church for Christian service after his ascension. The result of these gifts is to bring unity in the faith, a deeper knowledge of God and spiritual maturity. It is interesting to note that the gift of pastors is linked with the gift of teaching, and I believe this is significant because whilst the primary ministry of a pastor is to shepherd his flock, it is important that he will be able to teach and instruct his flock for works of service through his knowledge of God's word and its truth.

So, teachers and pastors go together inasmuch that a Pastor, through his teaching ability and discernment, should be able to be aware of the infiltration of false and heretical Bible teaching, recognised by those coming into the Church in the guise of what the Apostle Paul calls "ravaging wolves who will not spare the Flock" (Ephesians 20:28–31). In this same speech, Paul warns of members in the Church itself distorting the Scriptures and taking other members away from the fellowship to follow heresy and false teaching. Paul mentions in the same passage that for three years, he had never stopped warning the Ephesian Christians of such intrusions and had wept night and day with tears because of his shepherd heart and loving care for his flock. There is no doubt that pastors and overseers need the gifts of the Holy Spirit in these times as the early Church did then.

As Pastors and Shepherds, their primary responsibility is the safety and welfare of the Sheep. As we read the parable of the good shepherd in John's Gospel Ch 10, we see the measure of God's love as Jesus says, "I am the Good Shepherd who lays down his life for the Sheep." The care of the sheep is the shepherd's absolute priority, and Jesus gave his life for the sheep to save them from death. The cost and commitment of pastoral ministry in the light of Jesus' words as the good shepherd are very challenging indeed and make us aware of the formidable responsibility of such a calling. As with all the gifts, the all-important factor is the overriding fruit of love which should govern every motive and subsequent action in our service for Christ. For further understanding of a pastor's ministry, please refer to the notes on the gift of teaching, which, as mentioned at the beginning of this subject, is linked with pastoral ministry.

Pastors guide as well as feed the flock; cp Acts 20:28 with verse 17, which indicates this was the service committed to Elders (overseers or bishops). Also, in 1 Peter 5:1–2, "Tend the flock" involves tender care and vigilant superintendence.

Evangelists

(2 Tim Ch 4 v 5* Ephesians Ch 4 v11, Acts Ch 21 v 8)

There are only three verses in the whole of the Bible, which have the word 'evangelist' in them. That fact in no way diminishes the responsibility and importance of exercising the 'gift' of an evangelist, which means 'a messenger of good'. The Gospel of Jesus Christ is good news, and it comes from the Anglo-Saxon words 'god' = good and 'spell' = news. The gift is not mentioned in the list of the gifts of the Spirit in 1 Corinthians Ch 12 but is found in the epistle of Paul to the Ephesians 4:11.

Paul exhorts Timothy in his second epistle (above*) to do the work of an evangelist and to discharge all the duties of his ministry. Whilst preaching the Gospel is the duty of all Christians, and all believers should evangelise, the scriptures make it plain that some people have a 'special anointing' of the Spirit with respect to carrying out the work of an Evangelist. In Acts 21:8, Philip is given the title of an evangelist, quite specifically implying that it was a ministry for which he was well known and particularly gifted in.

Of course, it is a fact that all Christians should, at all times, be ready to give a reason for the hope that is within them (1

Peter 3:15), and Christ's commission to his eleven disciples in Matthew 28:19 would endorse the urgency of such a responsibility.

In Romans 10:14–15, Paul expresses his concern for his people Israel and reminds the Christian Jews of the importance of preaching the good news to them when he writes, "How will they hear without a preacher?"

As with all the gifts of the Spirit, they are only effective in accomplishing that for which they are given as they are used by those who have been baptised (filled) with the Spirit and so equipped for the particular ministry to which God has called them.

May we all remember that we are a "chosen people, a royal priesthood, a holy nation, a people belonging to God that we may declare the praises of him who brought us out of darkness into his wonderful light."

The great Prophet Isaiah speaks of our Lord, Jesus as the greatest Evangelist when he speaks of his Messianic ministry, which began with his anointing with the Holy Spirit to "preach good news to the poor." Etc. (Isaiah 61:1).

Helps (Those able to help others)

1 Cor Ch 12 v 28

Romans Ch 12 v 6–13

Many aspects of Christian service are highlighted in this passage, and each of us can identify with some of those areas of ministry to which the apostle draws our attention. As has been said throughout this series on the gifts of the Spirit, we all have different gifts, and the analogy of the Church as a 'body' is particularly relevant when we look at a list such as this. Each member of the 'body', as with the human body, has a specific function, and each part is vital to the satisfactory working of it in daily life.

'Helps' may be forthcoming in the form of serving, hospitality, financial support, encouragement, mercy, brotherly love, and prayers (Romans 12:6–13; 2 Cor 1:11).

Governments 1 Cor Ch 12
V 28 (Administration in Niv)

The Greek word *kubernesis* means to guide and denotes steering or piloting, and it is said of those who act as guides in a local church.

How vital in these days to have those in the Church who are able to get alongside their brothers and sisters in Christ to give them guidance and advice and to be able to steer them on the right course. Spiritual maturity and wisdom are pre-requisites to such a ministry, and with the breakdown of family life in some areas of society, many are bereft of parental guidance and stability. The first Epistle of John has much to commend it in its advice and admonition in relation to these gifts.

Prophets

(1 Cor Ch 12 Vs 27 – end)
(1 Cor Ch 14)

The Greek word means 'Public Expounder' (Ephesians 2:20).

It is helpful and important to understand that 'Prophecy' is God speaking to man whilst 'Tongues' is man speaking to God.

We are not dealing with the written prophesies of the Old Testament, nor are we concerned with the question of 'the last things' or the second coming of Christ, which things are sometimes called prophecy. By prophecy, we mean the occasional utterances given for the edification of the Church, which are seen in the Acts of the apostles and mentioned in the epistles. It is important that we understand this subject, for God has promised that in the last days, we shall hear more of these utterances (Acts 2:17–18; Joel 2:28–29; Acts 19:6).

Prophecy is a gift of the Holy Spirit and is a 'revelation' given by God about past, present or future matters. It is not always prediction or foretelling and is just as likely to be "forth-telling" (1 Cor 14:30). It is not preaching or teaching. To imagine that it leads to confusion.

Women are mentioned as having the gift of prophecy, and among them is Anna, who was a very devout lady and was continually in the temple and was known for her worshipping, fasting and praying; also, the four daughters of Philip, the evangelist, who are mentioned in Acts 21:8–9.

Agabus the Prophet first mentioned in Acts 11:27 predicted that a famine would spread over the entire Roman world. This did take place in the reign of Claudius (Acts 21:10–11) Agabus also prophesied the arrest of Paul by using the Apostle Paul's belt by tying his hands and feet with it and saying, "The Holy Spirit says, in this way the Jews of Jerusalem will bind the owner of this belt and will hand him over to the Gentiles." We know that this prophecy was fulfilled, and subsequently, Paul was arrested, and after facing Felix and Festus was sent to Rome.

Different Greek words are used for preaching, teaching and prophecy. However, prophecy may occur in preaching. That is, while a preacher is expounding the word of God, he may give him a fresh revelation about someone or something which he will pass on to the congregation. This is perhaps why some confuse prophecy with preaching and why some prophecy goes unrecognised.

Some revelations of the thoughts of a person's heart are sometimes mistakenly called 'a word of knowledge', but a careful study of the following scriptures indicate otherwise Luke 7:39 the prostitute who anointed Jesus' feet. The people commented that if Jesus had been a 'prophet', he would have known what sort of woman she was (John 4:18–19). Christ's knowledge that the woman at the well had had five husbands and the man she was now living with was not her husband.

Jesus exercised his 'prophetic' gift, and the Samaritan lady recognised that Jesus was truly a prophet (1 Cor 14:24–25).

In the church, whilst the gift is being used, a 'prophetic' revelation could reveal the secrets of a person's heart. This kind of revelation is always related to prophecy. There is not a single instance of such a revelation being called a word of knowledge in the whole of scripture. The 'word of knowledge' is related to teaching. It is the 'discourse' or 'utterance' of knowledge, a gift of the Holy Spirit which enables a man to plant spiritual knowledge in his hearers. Word of knowledge is more correctly rendered 'message of wisdom' and is related to teaching. 1 Cor Ch 2 gives us a greater insight into the gift of 'the message of knowledge'.

What is prophecy for? In 1 Corinthians 14:3, we are told that it is for edification, exhortation and comfort. Verse 4 goes on to say that it edifies the church. Sometimes this may consist in the revealing of the thoughts of the heart (1 Cor 14:24–25).

How should we react to prophecy?

a) We should not despise it but listen carefully to it (1 Thess 5:20).

b) Prophecy should be judged (1 Cor 14:29) and examined. Two or three prophets should speak, and the others should carefully weigh what has been said (1 Thess 5:21) and only that which is good held on to.

c) We must not try to 'winkle out' sins in ourselves. If a prophecy is for an individual, that person will know beyond any doubt that it is for him. Do not try to scrape together enough guilt to make it fit you, otherwise what God intends to edify could become condemnatory.

d) Even more important, we must try not to apply the prophecy to others. The devil is called "the accuser of the brethren" Rev 12:10, and if we sit smugly applying challenging prophecy to others, we are doing the devil's work. The Holy Spirit is perfectly capable of speaking to a person and convicting them without us trying to find a victim.

How should we judge prophecy?

a) Prophecy is always under the control of the prophet. He does not have to speak. 1 Cor 14:32 "The spirits of prophets are subject to the control of prophets."

b) Prophecy and any other ministry or participation must be controlled by the elders of the church (Acts 20:28–30; Titus 1:9–11).

c) Prophecy is to be judged in the light of Scripture (Isaiah 8:20 11 Tim 3:15, 4:4; Jer 14: 14).

d) All utterances must glorify Christ (1 Cor 12:3).

e) Prophecy should edify and bless the church (1 Cor 14:3,12). Good fruit is to be expected from true prophecy (Matt 7:15–20).

f) All gifts, including prophecy, must be governed by love (1 Cor 13).

g) A person who purports to prophesy should be living in obedience and submission to those over him in the Lord. "Is the prophet under authority"? (Luke 7: 8–9; 1 Peter 5:5).

h) Other Christians and especially other prophets, teachers, or leaders, are under an obligation to judge, weigh and consider Prophecy 1 Cor 14:29; 1 Thess 5:19–21.

i) The gift of discerning spirits is not only for recognising the presence of demons but also for discerning the authentic presence of the Holy Spirit and assessing the 'spirit' in which a prophecy is delivered (1 Cor 12:10).

j) In some cases, it may be necessary to "try the spirit" as in 1 John 4:1–3.

k) If predictive prophecy is uttered, the test of Deut 18:22 may be applied. (If a prophecy doesn't come to pass, then it cannot have come from God).

1. All Spirit-filled believers have the potentiality of that 'inner witness' of the Spirit whether something is right or not (1 John 2:20,27; Romans 8:16; Eph 4:72; Cor 10:12–18).

As mentioned at the beginning of this subject on the ministry of a prophet, emphasis is put on the use of this 'vital' gift which should be "eagerly desired" (1 Corinthians 14:1) inasmuch that the prophet "speaks to people for their strengthening, encouraging and comfort" (1 Corinthians 14:3). How important that men and women in the Church in these days should have a thirst for God's gifts, that in all things Christ may have the pre-eminence.

Teachers

1 Cor Ch 12 Vs 27 – end

Ephesians Ch 4 Vs 7–16

The Greek word used by the Apostle Paul in 1 Cor 12:28 and Ephesians 4:11 is '*didaskalos*', which means teacher or instructor. The title signifies the ability to be able to instruct and train God's people in the word of God and its teaching.

Once again, teaching is a gift of the Holy Spirit, but as with all the gifts, it is not a gift everybody has (1 Cor 12:29).

It is important that the leadership of the Church recognises the respective gifts of the Spirit and 'allows' them to be used for the edification of the body of Christ (Romans 12:7). All too often, there are too many square pegs in round holes!

The gift of teaching is a gift which may take time to manifest itself inasmuch that it comes with time spent in 'searching' the Scriptures and learning the deep things of God from teachers who have been anointed by the Spirit and have a sound grasp of the word.

The Hebrew Christians were challenged by the writer of the epistle to consider the fact that they should have grown sufficiently spiritually that they should have been able to exercise a 'teaching' ministry, but sadly, they had been slow to learn. They lacked understanding of some of the elementary truths of the scriptures and needed to learn them all over again (Hebrews 5:11 – end).

The greatest teacher of all is the Holy Spirit, and part of his work is to 'teach us all things', and as the Scriptures are God-breathed, the Spirit is able to help us to understand them and to be able to impart their truths to our brothers and sisters in Christ (John 14:23–26; 1 Cor Ch 2).

Jesus was, of course, a wonderful teacher, and throughout his short life, he was constantly teaching his disciples and the crowds (Matt 5 whole Chapter; Matt 4:23; and 9:35 etc.). He taught with divine authority, not like the teachers of the law who quoted other Rabbis to support their teaching. Jesus taught that his teaching was 'not his own' but that it had come from 'him who sent me' (John 7:16). Jesus was in constant communion with the Father, and his life was lived in obedience to his Father, and the words he taught were expressing the Father's heart and will to those with whom he came into contact.

So, in our own ministry, we should be listening to the Holy Spirit for his prompting that our teaching may be truly God-given and for his glory.

It is so important, that as believers, we should have a hunger for the word of God, and to this end, we should search the Scriptures and learn to "rightly divide the Word of Truth" (2 Tim 2:15). If we are going to grow in the knowledge of the Scriptures, we need men amongst us who are able to teach and instruct us in the things of God.

The Apostle Paul, before he became a Christian, was very well versed in the Old Testament, being a devout Pharisee having been taught by the most honoured Rabbi of the first century, a man by the name of Gamaliel (Acts 22:3). Being well versed in the Old Testament Scriptures stood him in very good stead when he became a Christian. He was able to see in all the Scriptures the 'things concerning Christ' from the prophetical writings and the typology of the temple worship with its animal sacrifices and so on. The 53rd chapter of Isaiah would certainly have been seen in a new light and other scriptures which he would have applied to the nation of Israel he now applied to the person of Jesus Christ, the Jewish Messiah (Luke 24:25–27). His insight into the Scriptures through his conversion and the ministry of the Holy Spirit enabled him to write so much of the New Testament through which he and his readers have been enlightened and taught regarding God's eternal purposes in Christ.

If it is possible to have a good grounding in the Scriptures from an early age, this contributes substantially in shaping our future knowledge and understanding of the word of God. Paul writing to Timothy reminds him of the 'sincere faith' which first lived in his mother Eunice and his grandmother Lois and which he persuaded now lives in Timothy himself (2 Tim 1:5).

In the Church, one of the many 'qualities' of an elder/overseer is to have the ability to teach, amongst other things. His desire to be an elder is described as a noble task. Other Spiritual qualities should also characterise such 'men', which are clearly listed in 1 Timothy 3:1–7.

The Apostles Paul and Barnabas were great teachers (Acts 11:25–26). At Antioch, they met with the church and taught great numbers of people for a whole year. Paul also spent a year and a half in Corinth teaching the word of God after the Lord had spoken to him in a vision to "keep on speaking and not be silent" (Acts 18:9–11). His teaching ministry was not limited to the church but was carried out in the homes of people whom he was seeking to win for Christ (Acts 20:20).

Paul said that he would rather speak five words of 'instruction' in the church than 10000 words in tongues (1 Cor 14:19).

Teaching carries with it great responsibilities, one of which is the practical outworking of the things in one's own life, which have been taught (1 Cor 4:17).

Sometimes we are called by God to preach his truth to specific people or nations which, of course, is part of the great commission. The Apostle Paul was called to teach the true faith to the Gentiles (1 Tim 2:7). He was called to suffer because of his faith and teaching (2 Tim 1:11–13).

He also exhorted Titus to instruct and teach God's people and employees how to live (Titus 2 whole chapter).

After Pentecost, the believers devoted themselves to the Apostle's teaching and to the fellowship, to the breaking of bread and to prayer (Acts 2:42).

The teacher's contribution to the 'affairs' of the Church, as with Apostles and Prophets, played a very important part, and their ministry extended to other areas of Church activity such as the commendation of other believers to specific work to which the Lord had called them (Acts 13:1–3).

In all things, we need to be reminded that all scripture is 'God-breathed' and is profitable for 'teaching' rebuking, correcting, and training in righteousness so that the man of God may be thoroughly equipped for every good work (2 Tim 3:16–17). To this end, it is essential that we need, with the Spirit's endowment to rightly divide the word of truth (2 Tim 2:15).

The New Testament also warns about false teachers infiltrating the Church in the last days, and we need spiritual discernment to recognise such teaching and bring correction and the truth so that such doctrine can be eradicated and not be allowed to spread like yeast throughout the fellowship (Acts 20:29 etc. 1 Tim 4; 1 Tim 6:3–10; 2 Tim 4:1–8).

The Gift of Speaking in Tongues

Acts Ch 1 Vs 4 and 5. Acts Ch 2 whole Chapter Acts Ch 10 (Vs 44–6)

Acts Ch 19 Vs 1–7

1 Cor Ch 12 V 10. Ch 13 V 1, Ch 14.

Speaking in tongues is a gift of the Holy Spirit, and the first time it took place was on the Day of Pentecost when 120 believers were waiting for the promised Holy Spirit to come upon them as a permanent possession and to experience the baptism in the Holy Spirit to equip them with 'power' for Christian service (Acts Ch 1 and 2).

Speaking in tongues, on and after the Day of Pentecost was the 'result' of being 'filled' with the Holy Spirit (Acts 2:4), as was the case of the Gentile believers in Acts 10:44–46 and the believers in Ephesus Acts 19:1–7. The fact that some Christians don't believe in the need for a 'personal' baptism in the Holy Spirit may account for the fact that they do not exercise some of the gifts of the Spirit as outlined by the Apostle Paul in 1 Cor Chapters 12, 13, and 14. Baptism in the Holy Spirit is not just a historical event into which all Christians are 'automatically' inaugurated through conversion, any more than are John's baptism of repentance and Christian baptism, which need to be experienced individually to have any significance or benefit.

What is "speaking in tongues"?

Paul calls it "speaking in different kinds of tongues" (1 Cor 12:10). This implies that as with the languages, which we speak on this earth, so with the "tongues of Angels" (Acts 13:1)., there are different 'languages'; they do not all sound the same!

So, putting it simply, when we speak in a tongue, we are speaking in a 'Heavenly' language, and that is the reason we need an interpreter because we are not in Heaven yet, and we need to know what we are saying to God. "For that is what tongues are; they are prayers to God" (1 Cor 14:2). We are not speaking to men but to God, and we are told that we are speaking 'mysteries'.

It would seem that speaking in tongues is 'primarily' for one's personal edification (1 Cor 14:4) as opposed to those who prophesy and edify the Church. However, if there is an interpretation of a tongue, the whole church will be edified (1 Cor 14:5). Nevertheless, Paul stresses the preference of prophesying, which is for the strengthening, encouragement, and edification of the whole church (1 Cor 14:3). It is important to note too that Paul mentions that a person praying in tongues privately should pray for an interpretation, for even in private, we should know what we have spoken so that we may be built-up and encouraged in our communion with the Lord (1 Cor 14:13–17). When we pray in a tongue, we pray 'in our spirit', but our mind is 'unfruitful', that is, we don't know what we are saying, and that is why it is imperative that we pray that God will give us the interpretation of what we have been saying. Tongues then are said to be unfruitful if we only pray in the spirit without interpretation.

Similarly, with 'singing' in tongues in the Church, unless there is interpretation, how can it be edifying to others and enable them to say 'Amen' if they have no idea what you're talking about! "They will not be edified or blest, and the exercise is unfruitful" (1 Cor 14:15–20).

To reiterate what was said earlier, tongues is '**speaking to God**' and not to men, and so it is important that we realise that we are never receiving some message for us from the Lord through a tongue so that it would seem that all prayers in tongues would be praise and worship as was the case on the day of Pentecost when the people heard the Christians "declaring the wonders of God in their own tongues" (Acts 2:11). I think it's important to note that on the day of Pentecost, no interpretation was necessary as the people understood what was being said in their own language.

Subsequently, when the gift of tongues was used in the Church, there was one notable difference, and that was the need for interpretation.

The Apostle Paul specifically mentions a 'separate' gift of "interpretation of tongues" (1 Cor 12:10)., although he doesn't dismiss the fact that the person with the gift of tongues can also have the gift of interpretation (1 Cor 14:13).

I am well aware that apparently there have been those who have been in a church abroad when a person has spoken in a 'tongue', and the congregation has understood what was said in their own language, without the need of an interpreter. I believe all things are possible but would prefer to address such a 'happening' as a 'miracle' rather than a 'speaking in tongues' in the way that the Apostle describes the way the gift of 'tongues' should operate in the church generally.

If, whilst someone is speaking in a tongue, a person 'senses' that God is wishing to speak to his people through a prophetic word, he/she should wait until an interpretation of the tongue has been given first. That prophetic word is NOT an interpretation of the tongue and should not be delivered until an interpretation has been given. It must be remembered that tongues are always man speaking to God and not God speaking to man.

Tongues should be used in an orderly manner, and the Apostle Paul clearly states that they should be used by two or at the most three, and each one must speak one at a time, and there must be an interpretation (1 Cor 14:27–28). Before proceeding with the service, there must be an interpretation, and if there isn't, the Scriptures imply that the person with the gift of tongues should remain silent and should speak to himself and God (1 Cor 14:28).

Tongues are given as a sign not for believers but unbelievers. However, it is imperative that they operate as directed by the apostle. Paul says that if an unbeliever comes into the Church and everybody is speaking altogether in tongues, he or she will say that "you are all out of your mind." In other words, it's not going to be the same as the Day of Pentecost, in fact, the opposite, so we need to heed this instruction, for there are some churches which operate this way (1 Cor 14:23–25).

Paul specifically says that he would rather speak five intelligible words in the Church than 10000 words in tongues (1 Cor 14:18–19). It's 500% more profitable if the Church knows what's being said, and that's why interpretation is essential.

Finally, the apostle says, "I would like every one of you to speak in tongues..." (1 Cor 14:5). He also adds, "Do not forbid speaking in tongues. But everything should be done in a fitting and orderly way" (1 Cor 14:39–40).

A solemn reminder to conclude:

"If I speak in the tongues of men and of Angels and have not love, I am only a resounding gong or a clanging cymbal" (1 Cor 13:1).

Jesus said, "A new commandment I give unto you that you love one another as I have loved you" (John 13:34).

A Prayer for The Holy Spirit's Anointing

Words and Music by Lyall Drewett

Holy Spirit come and cleanse us, fill our hearts anew
Bring your sanctifying power, fill us through and through
Pour your gifts of grace upon us, show us Christ alone
Glorify the name of Jesus, he is Lord alone

Jesus Christ to us so precious, risen Glorious King
All our praise and humble worship now to you we bring
Fill our lives, renew our minds, take all our sin away
May the Prince of Power and Glory all his gifts display

May we know the Spirit's unction, let us see the Lord
He who died and now is risen, Christ the Living Word
May our hearts adore and worship, he who reigns above
He who with the Glorious Father is the King of Love.

Lyall Drewett

59